Minding Minutes with Minute Minders

More than 150 Activities to Stimulate Creative Thinking

by
Troy W. Cole

illustrated by June Kern Weber

Cover by Tom Sjoerdsma

Copyright © 1994, Good Apple

ISBN No. 0-86653-795-3

Printing No. 98765432

Good Apple
1204 Buchanan St., Box 299
Carthage, IL 62321-0299

Paramount Publishing

Acknowledgments

This book is dedicated to
Betty J. Cole

for correcting my spelling,
putting the punctuation in all the right places,
and making my words make sense.
Most important of all, she created the expression
"Minute Minders" and gave it to me to use just 'cause
she likes and loves me

and

to all the teachers and students who
enjoy minding minutes with "Minute Minders."

Preface

Through the largeness of things
        there are basic cores,
And within these cores
        are simple and quiet truths.
Like Buckminster Fuller's construct
        of doing more with less,
in this book we share what is simple,
        what is basic, what is essential,
and what is true.

                                Bob Stanish

GA1489

Foreword

I have been writing "Minute Minders" for *Challenge* magazine for several years. Many teachers and students have shared with me how much they enjoy thinking about and doing them.

In this book I have expanded "Minute Minders" for your challenge and pleasure. Most of the ideas are new, but I have also included and expanded a few of my old favorites.

Use this book to fill the vacant moments that occasionally occur in school. Have fun as you think and think as you have fun.

Troy

GA1489

Minding Minutes with Minute Minders

This book is for thinking.

Thinking is . . .
    using one's mind,
      using one's intellect,
        productive, natural,
          stimulating, and essential.
It is the birthplace of ideas,
    the essence of imagination,
      the beginning of curiosity,
        and the cradle of creativity.

Table of Contents

GA1489

About This Book

Minding Minutes with Minute Minders is a book for teaching, thinking, learning, and doing. It is a book of challenging activities that are designed to nurture creativity, accommodate modality, and stimulate whole mindedness.

This book gives students and teachers an opportunity to think divergently and convergently and to apply the creative problem-solving skills of brainstorming, elaborating, enhancing, synthesizing, and choosing.

Each activity is presented to stimulate and practice creative thinking and encourage fluency, flexibility, elaboration, and originality. Many of the activities also involve personal choice and valuing. When minding minutes with minute minders, remember these simple rules: accept responses, encourage participation, and defer judgement.

Minding Minutes with Minute Minders is also a book designed for enjoyment. It should be lots of fun. It gives teachers and students an opportunity to think about, imagine, and accept the uncommon. An uncommon sense is special and should be developed, used, guided, and appreciated.

This book is written to fill those times when teachers need and want to provide something to do that is exciting, challenging, creative, and productive.

Enjoy *Minding Minutes with Minute Minders.*

Setting the Setting
for
Minding Minutes with Minute Minders

For the most productive use of this book, a learning climate should be established to:

- stimulate idea production

- provide ample think-response time

- ignite originality and humor

- stress open, accepting idea exchange

- cause transformations and experimentation

- encourage flexibility and elaboration

- practice visualization and imaging

- allow and structure cooperative products

- be warm, caring, accepting, and exciting

Now
it
is
time
to
begin.

GA1489

Thinking About Clocks and Time

1

GA1489

Clocks and Time

Time is the fortune of life,
   the architect of being.
Time is all dreams, desires,
   hopes and expectations.
Time is rich and poor, powerful and humble,
   strong and weak, apparent and obscure.
Time is memories, delights,
   joys and happiness.
Time is the inflicter and the healer.

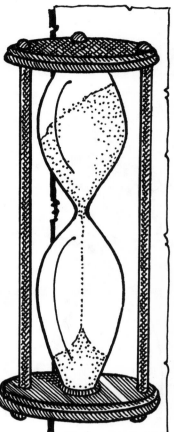

Time is
spent
saved
wasted
conserved
lost
questioned
answered
and told.

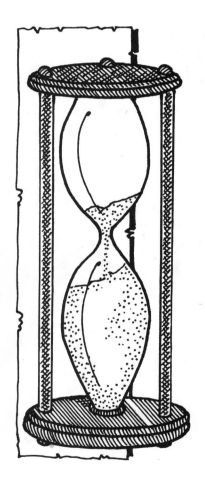

Time is
your time
my time
our time
work time
playtime
time out
didn't-have-the-time
and just-messing-around time.

Time is an instant
and forever,
a feeling, a glimpse,
a thought, a touch,
a hug and a smile.
Quickly it comes. Quickly it goes.

Time was. Time is. Time will be.
The only caretaker of my time is me.

TC

GA1489

Time for . . .

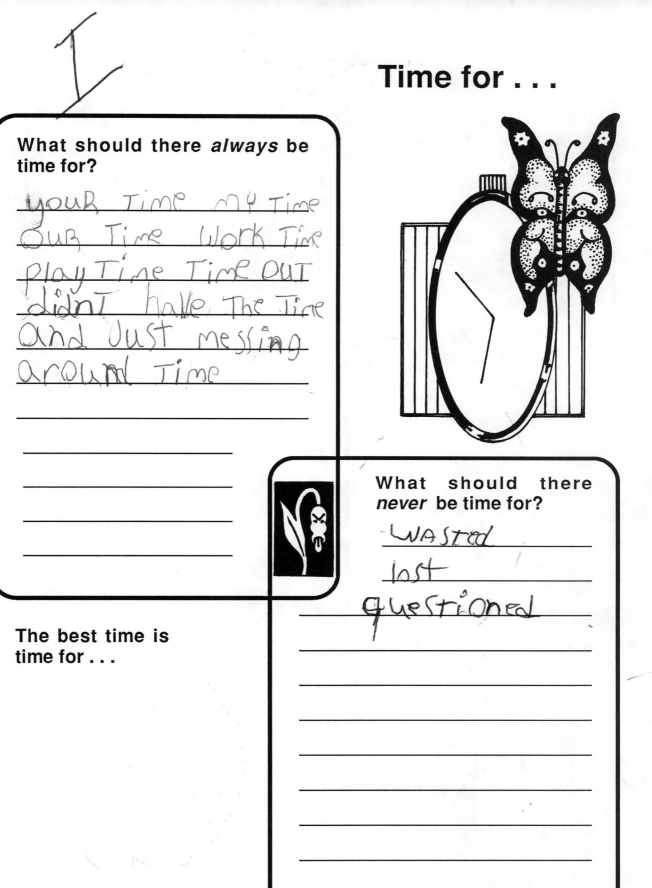

What should there *always* be time for?

your time my time
our time work time
play time time out
didnt have the time
and just messing
around time

The best time is time for . . .

What should there *never* be time for?

wasted
lost
questioned

3

Ticktock

What would fit between a tick ½ se

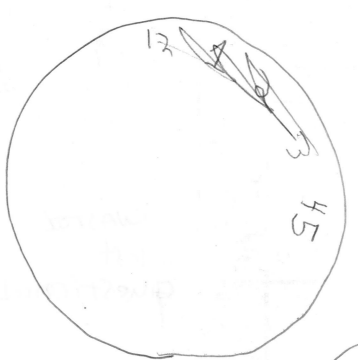

and a tock?

Clockaphelia—Clockaphobia

Why might

Sam say he loves clocks? Cas He Dose   **Sam say he hates clocks?** No

How do you feel about clocks? OoK

5

GA1489

Imagine a conversation between a clock and a carrot. Choose a partner. One be the clock; one be the carrot. Have a two-minute conversation.

Some other things with which a clock could have a conversation are a carburetor, clarinet, cloud, caterpillar, or a cutie pie.

Draw some clocks doing unusual things.

GA1489

Time Quicks

A quiet time is . . .

A peaceful time is . . .

A noisy time is . . .

A loud time is . . .

A good time is . . .

A happy time is . . .

A busy time is . . .

A slow time is . . .

A bad time is . . .

A beautiful time is . . .

A _____ time is . . .

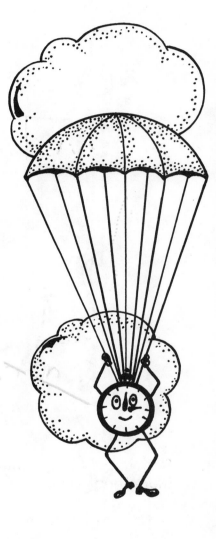

Hint: Substitute colors, sizes, shapes, and metals as descriptive words.

GA1489

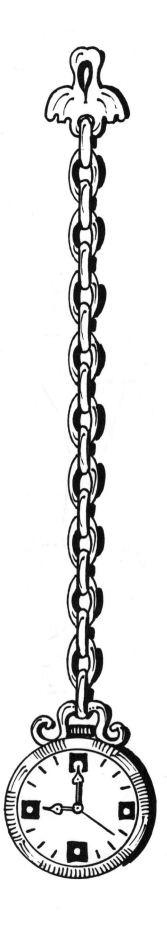

Saving Time

Pretend that you could save time up
to use another day,
to use in any way you want,
to work, to sleep, to read, to play.

You can save it in a bottle, a box, a can
or a jar with a fancy lid.
That you can make the time and take the time
and keep it safely hid.

Putting time pennies in a piggy bank
each minute adding more.
Sixty minutes put away, an hour,
a day, still more.

Where would you keep your saved-up time?
What would you keep it in?
Where would you hide your cache of time?
How did your saving begin?

When will you open your stored-away time?
What will you use it for?
When the time you've saved is all used up,
how will you then get more?

TC

GA1489

Saving Time

If I pretend to save time up
to use in my own way,
I would save it up until

_____.

I would put it in a _____
all sealed up good and tight.
I would hide it _____

_____.

I would only open my cache of time

_____.

I would use my stored-up time

_____.

When the time is all used up
as it's often been before,
I'll _____
That will get me more.

By _____

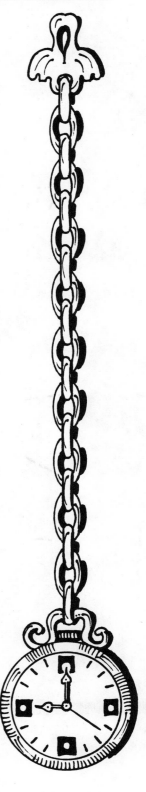

Time poem response.
Fill in the spaces.
Make a time rhyme.

GA1489

This page is for drawing clocks, writing poems about time, or spending some time doing something you enjoy.

Imagine spinning a time wheel. When would you want it to start and where would you want it to stop?

Thinking

About

Letters

and

Words

BCDEFGHIJKLMNOPQRSTUVWXYZ

GA1489

Letters and Words

To Students:

Letters make words. Words are powerful, wonderful, beautiful, amazing, delightful, and funny. Words make us feel happy, sad, angry, and caring. Words paint pictures in our minds and express our ideas. They can say "I like and love you." They can make us laugh. They can rule a country. Words. Enjoy them.

To Teachers:

Language is a structure built with letters, sounds, and gestures that become words—that become thoughts—that become ideas—that become a foundation of existence. The language process may be as important as the product. Some students may have difficulty with school language, but have an appreciation for and enjoy the use of language.

Having fun with words and removing the fear from language is in part the intent of this unit. An attitude toward language can be nurtured in the classroom. The activities are designed to encourage students to think about and explore letters and words in a new and different way.

An Abbreviated Story: The Process and the Product

I have never learned to read very well. I can't spell, punctuate, nor do I know or practice rules of grammar. I had a miserable school experience as a result of it. I did, however, know from early on that I like words. I loved poetry, to be read to, and to hear and tell stories. I kept special words and poems and stories in my head. They were safe from school there because they had no school way out.

Now, at last, some of the words are finding a way out. Encouragement from special people and excellent careful editing make it possible for me to be a writer. The words, ideas, and stories have always been there. It was the process that I was missing.

Troy W. Cole

GA1489

Letter Quicks

If you were to choose a letter for a pet, which would you pick?

Which letter is

busiest? _____

dullest? _____

happiest? _____

healthiest? _____

loneliest? _____

prettiest? _____

proudest? _____

saddest? _____

strongest? _____

weakest? _____

If the letters had a popularity contest, which letter would you choose

to win? ➝ ◯

to place second? ➝ ◯

to be last? ➝ ◯

What letter is the most fun to say?

_____

One bright sunny day
A met R to go and play.
A suggested that they find E
So they would then be three.
They found E and now are three.
They're A, R, E.
The three that make ARE be.

Think of another three-letter word.
Use its letters in this rhyme.
You may wish to be adventurous
and try a four- or five-letter word in
your rhyme.

GA1489

Use this page for decorating letters or decorating with letters.

Hint: Make your initials with fancy letters.

A, H, K, L, M, N, V, X, Z

Use your imagination and combine any or all of these letters to draw a bridge across the stream.

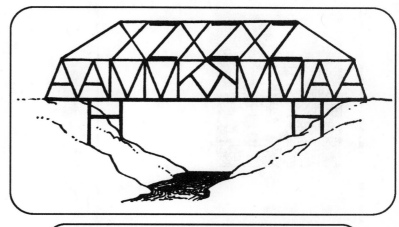

Hint: You may rotate the letters. Make them larger or smaller. Use lines to join them.

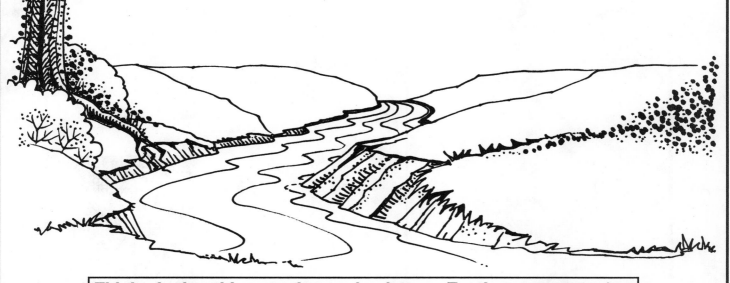

Think of other things to draw using letters. Try them. ➡

15

This page is for creating picture words, writing shadow words, and drawing designs with letters and words.

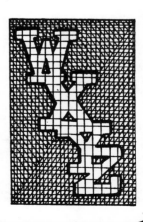

GA1489

A B C D E F G H I J K L M N O P Q

R
S
T
U
V
W
X
Y
Z

Q is
my friend.

Imagine the alphabet
lined up from a to z
waiting to make words
anxiously.
If letters have feelings
like you and me,
where on this continuum
would each letter be?

a
b
c
d
e
f
g
h
i
j
k
l
m
n

◄Happy————————Okay————————Sad►

Explain why you placed some of the letters where you did.

But I'm
never alone.

o p q r s t u v w x y z

17

A Word List

Glisten
Glistener
Glistening
Glistens

Gleam
Gleamer
Gleaming
Gleams

Glimmer
Glimmerer
Glimmering
Glimmers

Gurgle
Gurgler
Gurgling
Gurgles

Activities follow ⟶

GA1489

Glisten, Gleam, Glimmer, and Gurgle

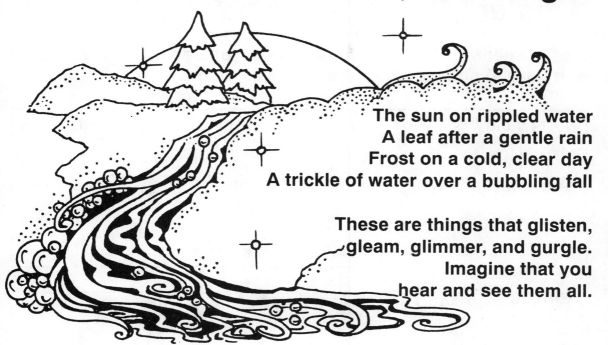

The sun on rippled water
A leaf after a gentle rain
Frost on a cold, clear day
A trickle of water over a bubbling fall

These are things that glisten,
gleam, glimmer, and gurgle.
Imagine that you
hear and see them all.

List things that:

Glisten	Gleam	Glimmer	Gurgle
_____	_____	_____	_____
_____	_____	_____	_____
_____	_____	_____	_____
_____	_____	_____	_____
_____	_____	_____	_____
_____	_____	_____	_____

Compare your list with a partner.
How many are different?
How many are the same?
How many fit on more than one list?

More ➡

GA1489

More
Glisten, Gleam, Glimmer, and Gurgle

Use the words that you think fit best (glisten, gleam, glimmer, and gurgle) and complete the activities below.

A new car _____ s.   A puppy _____ s.

An old toy _____ s.   A shared secret _____ s.

A new friend _____ s.   Money _____ s.

A good idea _____ s.   Love _____ s.

A_____ _____ s.   Happiness _____ s.

Write a sing-song sentence using all four words.

A _____ er   A _____ er

A _____ er   A _____ er

In the morning I _____.

In the evening I _____.

At school I _____.

At play I _____.

At home I _____.

On Saturday I _____.

GA1489

More Activities with Words

Building Word Trees

Choose a base word and build a word tree. Use words that you associate with the word.

Example

Vertical Word	Horizontal Word

```
 li G ht              s   f
    L augh            n   e
mell O w              u   e   s
    W hite            G   L   O   W
                      g   f   o
                      l   t   r
                      e       m
```

Note: This activity is known as acrostics, and it develops associational fluency.

Ranking

Rank these from *like most* to *like least*.

• things that gleam
• things that glisten
• things that glitter
• things that gurgle

_____

_____

_____

_____

Choose words from this unit and/or make your own list of alliterations to expand or change any activity on this page.

Draw a glistening, gleaming, glittering, gurgling picture here; or write a poem.

GA1489

Why Was I Late Today?

Well—you see— today
I met a squishy, squashy, squiggly, squirmy thing
while on my way to school.
It asked if I would stop and play.
I said, "No! No way.
I'll be late and that's against school rule."

I hurried along.
It followed me.
I stopped and turned and said,
"No, shoooo, scat, skidadel. Don't follow me.
I'm on my way to school."

But follow me it would and did.
Again I stopped and firmly said,
"I don't know what you are or who."

"Oh, I'm a soft and squishy, squashy, sqiggly, squirmy thing
and I'm often late for school."

After a pause,
     and a longer pause
          it looked me through and through.

Then it said,
     "I think . . .
          perhaps . . .
               that you just might be too!"

TC

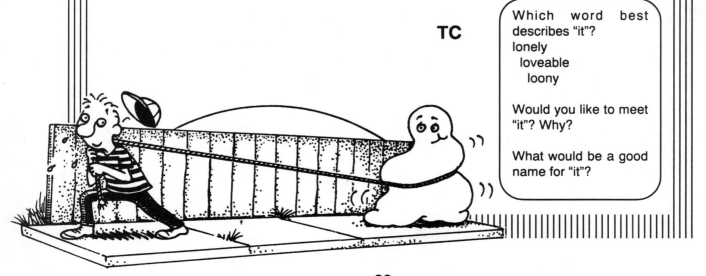

Which word best describes "it"?
lonely
  loveable
    loony

Would you like to meet "it"? Why?

What would be a good name for "it"?

22

GA1489

Another Word List

Three words and two blanks appear under each word. Fill each blank with a new word by adding a different ending. *Some of these words may not be in your dictionary, but you will be able to define them.*

Squishy

- Squishing
- _____
- Squisher
- _____
- Squish

Squashy

- Squash
- _____
- Squashing
- _____
- Squasher

Squiggly

- Squiggle
- _____
- Squiggler
- _____
- Squiggling

Squirmy

- Squirmer
- _____
- Squirm
- _____
- Squirming

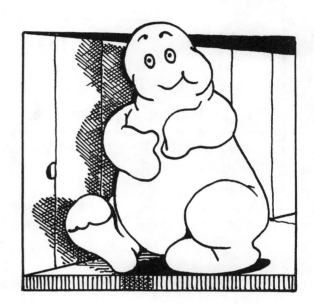

Add another word to the list.

Add five more.

- _____
- _____
- _____
- _____
- _____

23

GA1489

Squishy, Squashy, Squiggly, Squirmy Things

Things that are squishy are

_____, _____, and _____.

Things that are squashy are

_____, _____, and _____

Things that are squiggly are

_____, _____, and _____.

Things that are squirmy are _____, _____, and _____.

Name squishy things that you can hold in your hand.	Draw squashy things that are tiny.
Think about squiggly things that you like to touch.	What squishy, squashy, squiggly, squirmy things would Sam carry in his pocket?

Another List

Helpful
Help
Helping
Helper

Hopeful
Hope
Hoping
Hopeful

Humorous
Humor
Humoring
Humorist

Happy
Happiness
Happening
Happily

Absolutely Ecstatic

Choose a word from the list and draw a picture of it.

My picture is about

_____.

GA1489

Playing with the Happy Words

Definitions with a Difference

Example: Helpful is pulling sinking Sam out of slushy, soft quicksand.

Helpful is _____
_____.

Hopeful is_____
_____.

Humorous is _____
_____.

Happy is _____
_____.

Think of people you know who are helpful, hopeful, humorous, and happy. Make a list of things that make them that way.

Choose the word that best describes you:

• early in the morning.   Happy

• before lunch at noon.   Humorous

• just after school in the afternoon.   Helpful

• before going to bed at night.   Hopeful

Draw a line connecting the time with the word.

Are there more "H" words that could fit on this list?

GA1489

Words

Words paint pictures in our minds;
  they may be harsh, they may be kind.
There are words that make us laugh or cry,
  urge us to quit, encourage us to try.
Some words make us catch our breath,
  while others frighten us half to death.
It takes words to make a poem or song;
  and too many words make a book too long.

We use words exactly as they are
  or sometimes make'm up.
Often when we need to use them most

We forget,

hes - - - itate,

s–s–stutter

or

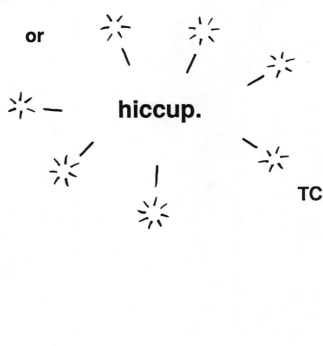

hiccup.

TC

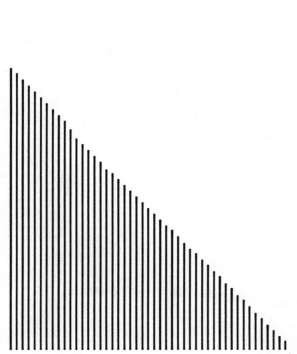

What are some more things words can do?

GA1489

Think of all the things you might do with words.
Choose one or two and use this page to start.

28

Unit 3

Thinking About Numbers, Shapes, and Solutions

GA1489

Numbers

0   This is zero.

1   This is one.

10   This is ten.

100   This is one hundred.

1,000   This is one thousand.

100,000   This is one hundred thousand.

1,000,000   This is one million.

1,000,000,000   This is one billion.

1,000,000,000,000   This is one trillion.

On it goes until we get to a googol. A googol is a 1 followed by 100 zeroes.

This is a googol. 10,000,000,000,000,000,000,000,000,000,000,000,
000,000,000,000,000,000,000,000,000,000,000,000,000,000,000,
000,000,000,000,000,000.

If you add 2 more zeroes to the googol you have a septendecillion. That's a 1 with 102 zeroes. Add 8, and you have an octodecillion with 108 zeroes; add 14 and get a novemdecillion with 114 zeroes; and add 20 to get a vigintillion with 120 zeroes. A centillion is a 1 followed by 600 zeroes. (I would not like to write a centillion, would you?)

The number system is very interesting and sometimes complex. You may wish to explore it more. Your dictionary may have a numbers table. There may be some books about numbers in your library.

By the way, for number nuts, the googol is not the largest number. We can go to a googolplex. A googolplex is a one with a googol of zeroes. Then there is probably a googolplex plexed. It makes some of us dizzy just thinking about numbers, while others love them.

Let's think some more about numbers.

30

GA1489

Number, Time, and Distance Statements

There are things that we hear and say that just aren't exactly so.

For instance:

If I've told you once, I've told you _____ times.

I'll be with you in a _____.

There must have been a _____ people there.

This is the _____ time I've tried this.

If you don't stop that this _____, I'm going to . . .

It won't take but a _____.

A _____ more _____ and we will be _____.

Have you ever heard someone say, "It's only a hop, skip and a _____ from here to there"?

Fill in the blanks above. Then think of more.

_____

_____

_____

_____

_____

_____

_____

_____

_____

_____

Why do you think we say things we may not mean?

31

GA1489

Number Quicks

What is your favorite number?

What number is most popular?

What number would you most like
to hold in your hand?

What number means the most to you?

What number does Sam dislike?

List three of the strongest numbers.

What number is prettiest?

List car numbers.

What number is the most dishonest or deceptive?

What do you most like to do with numbers?

Create magic telephone numbers and explain what they would do.

According to number historians, the last number to be created was zero. Think about numbers without the zero. How does zero change things? Explain.

Rank each of these using the numbers from 1 (like least) to 10 (like most).
__ playtime   __ work time   __ free time
__ books   __ balls   __ bubbles
__ bouncing   __ babbling   __ bronco
__ broccoli   __ babies   __ broke

What number could be used to design
__ a swing   __ a chair   __ a desk
__ a ball bat   __ a golf club   __ a pizza
__ a pair of sunglasses __ a doorknob   Others?

32

GA1489

Guessing

(Usually Called Estimating)

How far?

- Name something that is a block from your school.

- Name something that is about a mile from your school.

- Name something that is about 100 miles from your school.

- My home is about _____ from my school.

- Outer space is about _____ miles from my school.

How much?

- A new television will cost between $ _____ and $ _____.

- A new car will cost between $ _____ and $ _____.

- A new stereo will cost between $ _____ and $ _____.

- A horse will cost between $ _____ and $_____.

- A turkey for Thanksgiving will cost between $ _____ and

  $_____.

- A new _____ will cost between $_____ and $_____.

- If I had about $_____ I would buy _____.

- I have only $_____ so I am going to _____

  _____.

List some ways that you could check your estimates.

GA1489

List different ways to describe size.

_____

_____

_____

_____

_____

How big was it?

What size

are your shoes?

is your ring finger?

is your coat?

is your waist?

is your hat or cap?

are you?

is your family?

is your city or town?

is your state?

is _____?

Describe the size

of love.

of a dream.

of nothing.

of winning.

of waiting.

of wanting.

of friendship.

of goodbye.

GA1489

Distance and Direction

What is near yet far?

How do you get from there to here?

When can up be down?

What things are often "out of sight, out of mind"?

?? ?? Is it possible to be in two places at once?
Most of the time we are in many places at once.

List the places you are now.

_____

_____

_____

List a place *(with places)* you would like to be.

_____

_____

_____

Examples:

I am in my office, in my house, near Edwardsville, in Madison County, in the state of Illinois, in the United States, etc.

GA1489

Tricks of Nine

If nine had a shoe, what color would that shoe be?

Answer Check

Did you know that when you multiply any number by 9 the digits in the answer always add up to equal 9?

Try it.
$3 \times 9 = 27 \ldots 2 + 7 = 9$

This works for large numbers too.
$9 \times 42 = 378 \ldots 3 + 7 + 8 = 18$
$\ldots 1 + 8 = 9$

Finger Multiply

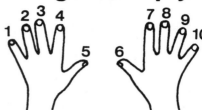

Put your hands in front of you and count your fingers from left to right. Bend the finger that you are multiplying by 9.

For example: To solve $2 \times 9 = ?$, bend finger #2. Then count the fingers on the left side of the bent finger. This is the first digit in the answer. (1)

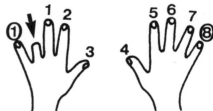

Then count the fingers on the right side of the bent finger. This is the second digit in the answer. (8)
Combine the digits from left to right, and the solution is $2 \times 9 = 18$.

Now try $7 \times 9 =$

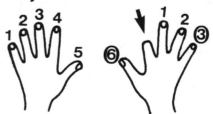

The solution for 7×9 is 63. Do some more.

Solutions

Write a question for each solution below.

One. No more, no less.

777

10101

161 or 100

364 or 366, but not 365

between one foot and a yard

$25,000 and some change

never more than an hour

one mile, four yards, two feet,
three and one-half inches

a rectangle and four circles

a top, a bottom, and only two sides

true most of the time, but there are exceptions

Shapes

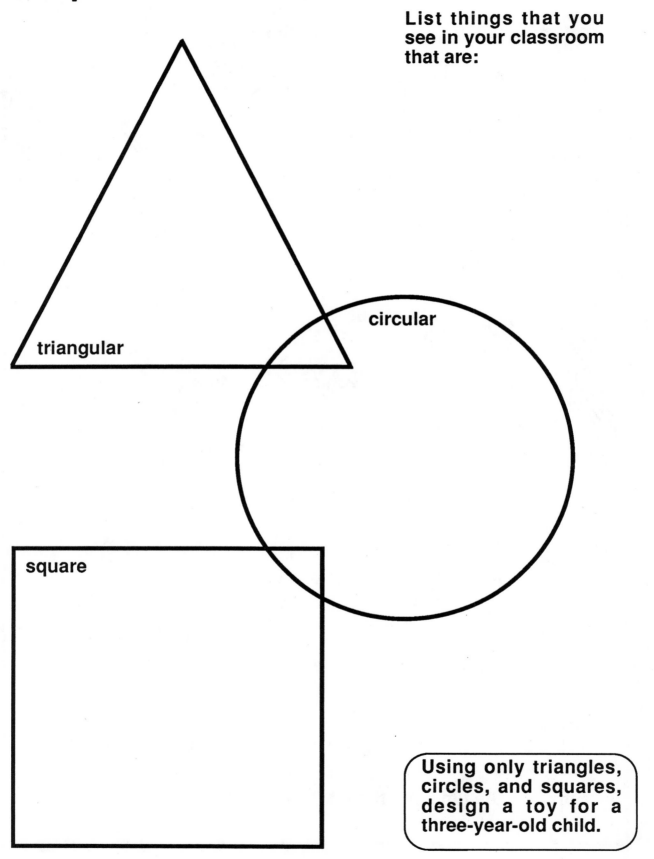

triangular

circular

square

Using only triangles, circles, and squares, design a toy for a three-year-old child.

38

Shapes Extended

Triangle, rectangle, polygon, circle, and square are a few of the many shapes that exist. Shapes are everywhere and some are often unnoticed. Let's think of shapes in a different way.

What shape do you think should be

the happiest?

painted red?

used for a secret hiding place?

most popular?

never seen?

always taken on a vacation?

important to birds?

lost then found?

used in a song?

changed?

the most important in everyone's life?

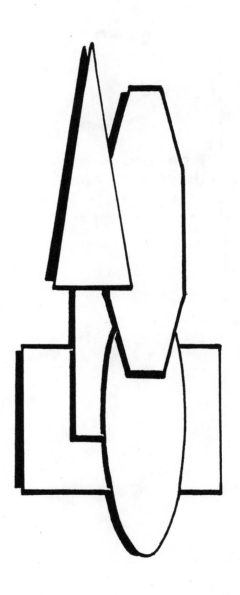

8 Face

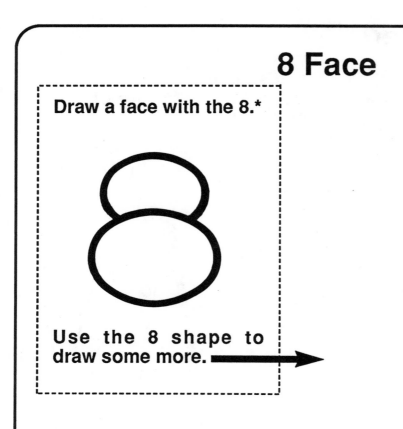

Draw a face with the 8.*

Use the 8 shape to
draw some more. ➡

*From: *Figure 8 Animals*, Troy W. Cole, Good Apple, 1993, GA1439.

40

GA1489

Thinking About Holidays and Celebrations

41

Holidays and Celebrations

Since people began to think, perhaps even before, there have been special days set aside for celebrating and resting. These early set-aside days are the ancestors of modern holidays and celebrations.

Holidays and celebrations occur to commemorate a variety of events. Among these events are the following:

Birthdays
Anniversaries
Planting
Harvesting
Discoveries
Freedom
Independence
Religious celebrations
Conquests
Astronomical occurrences
Wars
Spring breaks

Discovering the origin and purpose of each holiday is interesting and sometimes intriguing.

In most societies, holidays and celebrations are established by the government or by religion.

Holidays are significant to our heritage and for the most part have been established to celebrate that heritage.

GA1489

Holiday Quicks

If you could declare a new holiday, what would it be?

New holiday's name _____

New holiday's purpose _____

_____

_____

_____

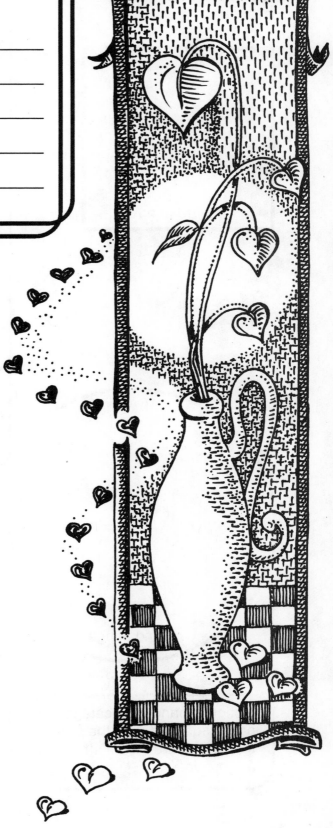

What color should the following be?

Independence Day

New Year's Day

Thanksgiving Day

Arbor Day

Christmas Day

Hanukkah

Halloween

Valentine's Day

Easter

Choose one of these holidays and list five words that describe it.

43

GA1489

Holiday Word Association

Write the name of a holiday in the octagon. Name things that are square, rectangular, round or triangular that you associate with that holiday.

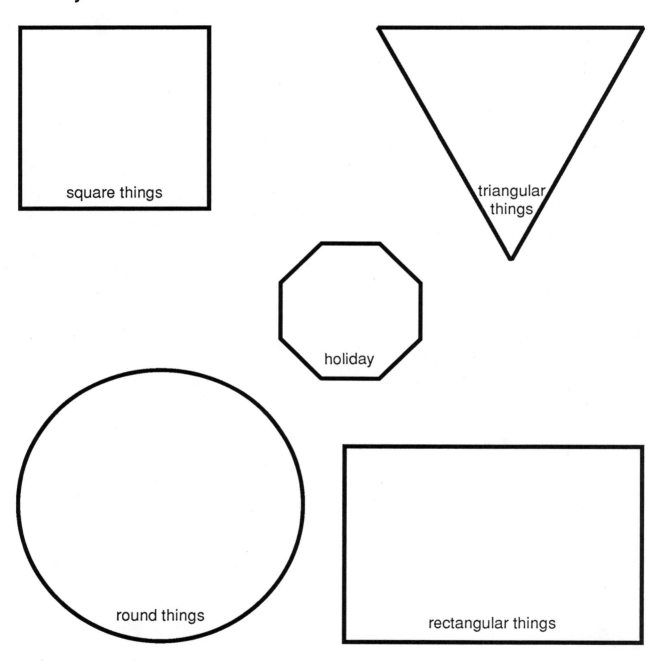

square things

triangular things

holiday

round things

rectangular things

Option: Change the categories from shapes to colors. (For example, list things that are associated with the holiday—in the square, things that are red; in the triangle, things that are blue; in the circle, things that are green; in the rectangle, things that are brown.

Celebration

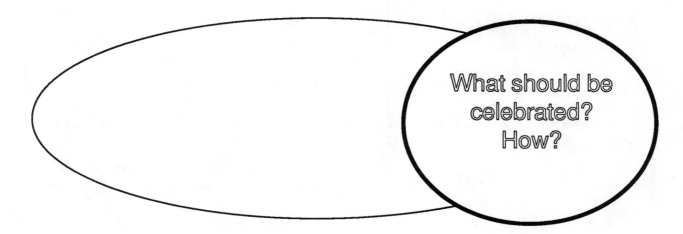

What should be celebrated? How?

Describe a national Howdy Do Day.

Shhhhhh! What sounds might be heard during a worldwide no-talking day?

Create a "The Best
Things in Life Are
Free" Day.

Describe a celebration
of the most beautiful
things in the world.

Your town should be
known as the _____
capital of the world.

What flower would
best represent a
National Flower Day?

Combine three of your favorite things and tell how they
could be celebrated together.

GA1489

Thinking About The Strange and Unusual

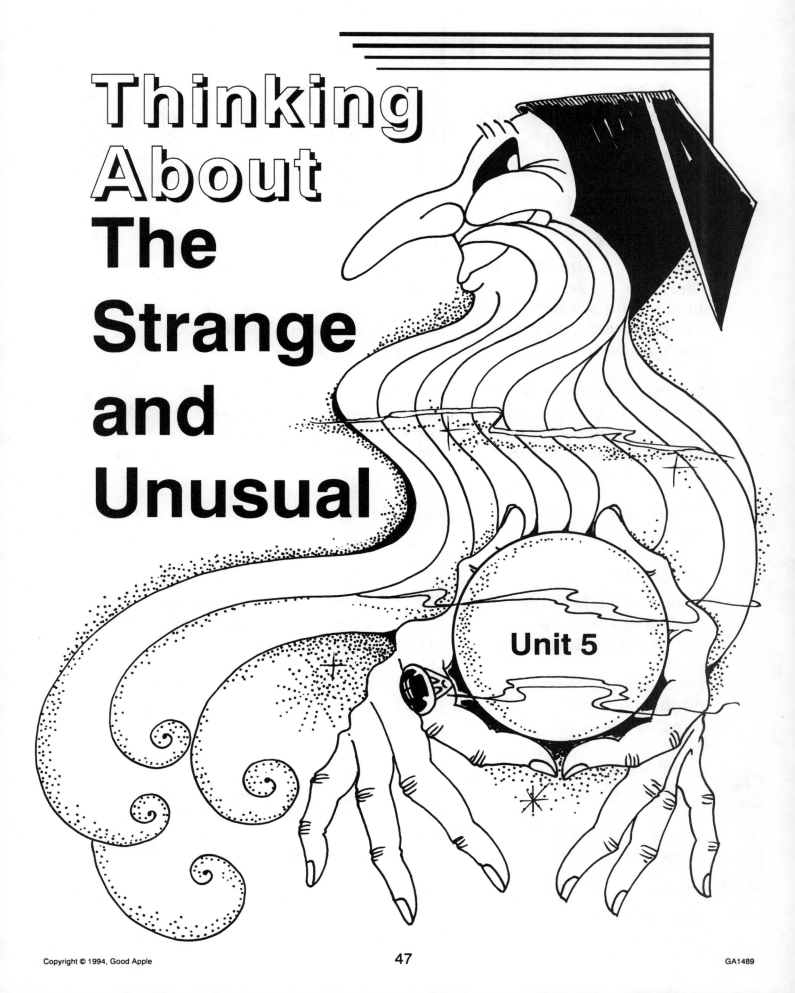

Unit 5

The Strange and Unusual

To Students:

In this unit strange, unusual, and imaginary images are presented. You are encouraged to be as creative and original as you can possibly be. Let your imagination go. Don't be critical of your ideas. Play with them, embellish and enhance them. You may be surprised and enjoy where they will take you. Most of all have fun!

To Teachers:

In this unit strange, unusual, and imaginary images are the focus. They are presented to encourage imagining, enhance flexibility, and involve the students in mind-play. A structure for creativity is provided. However, you may need to begin by saying "what about . . ." or "let's consider . . ." or "in what ways . . . ," etc.

Some students may still be hesitant to become involved. Let those who are eager and enjoy using their imaginations take the lead. The more reserved students will provide an interesting balance. If some students prefer not to think about strange and unusual things, that's okay too.

Remember to look for and encourage flexiblity, elaboration, and originality.

Suggestion:

Some of the activities in this unit are designed as individual exercises. Others will work well as partner or small group activities. A few may work best when presented to the whole class.

Producing, accepting, and sharing a variety of ideas will help students gain insight into and participate comfortably in creative and imaginative activities.

Other uses:

- Art and Drawing

- Interest Centers

- Research and Resource Use (What is known about wizards, space, etc.?)
- Drama and Playacting

GA1489

What
could
these
wizards
do with
a wok
a toc
a rock
and
a clock?

49

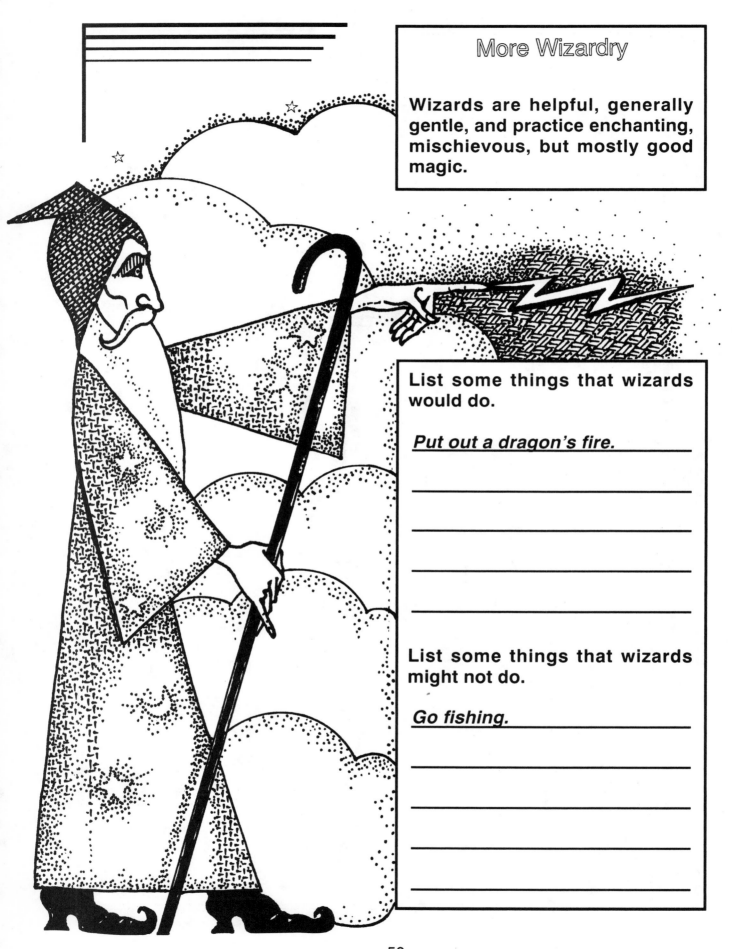

More Wizardry

Wizards are helpful, generally gentle, and practice enchanting, mischievous, but mostly good magic.

List some things that wizards would do.

Put out a dragon's fire.
_____
_____
_____
_____
_____

List some things that wizards might not do.

Go fishing.
_____
_____
_____
_____

50

GA1489

On this page write a story, poem, or song about a wizard, a princess, an evil oracle, a confused dragon, and a journey to the lost castle.

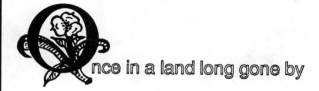 nce in a land long gone by

Didja

Didja ever look at the starry sky
and wonder what lay beyond
all those wispy lights you see
and those that are long since gone?

Didja ever see the moon shining at day
and wonder where the stars are hidden away
or scheme a trip through and beyond
that place where nothingness and silence
belong?

There is a place
just for you and me
when we persist
and dream travelers be.

TC

This is a silent space.

This is a silent space.

Say What?

Choose one: **Then**   **Choose one:**

- A boomawhat

- A monoculaped
  (has one eye and one foot)

- A nonacartrex
  (a newly discovered dinosaur)

- A nolter
  (discovered in the high
  Himalaya Mountains)

- A tigator
  (half tiger, half alligator)

- A hippoflea

- Create your own.

- Draw it.

- Write a poem about it.

- Describe it.

- Give it a common name and explain.

- Think of a safe hiding place for it.

- Devise a way to disguise and secretly transport it.

- Think of fun things you could do with it.

After choosing, write or draw here.

53

GA1489

An Anachronoid

You have an anachronoid.

- What is it?
- What can it do?
- Where did it come from?
- How did it get here or there?
- Do you like it?
- What do you like or not like to do with it?
- Does anything make it malfunction? What?

Create a story about you and your anachronoid shopping in a supermarket.

My Anachronoid and Me

GA1489

What If . . .

pencils and pens had built-in mistake detectors?

remote controls had beepers that would help you locate them when they were misplaced?

cars could drive themselves?

eggplants had real eggs, beefsteak tomato plants produced real beefsteaks, and money did grow on trees?

55

GA1489

Again, What If . . .

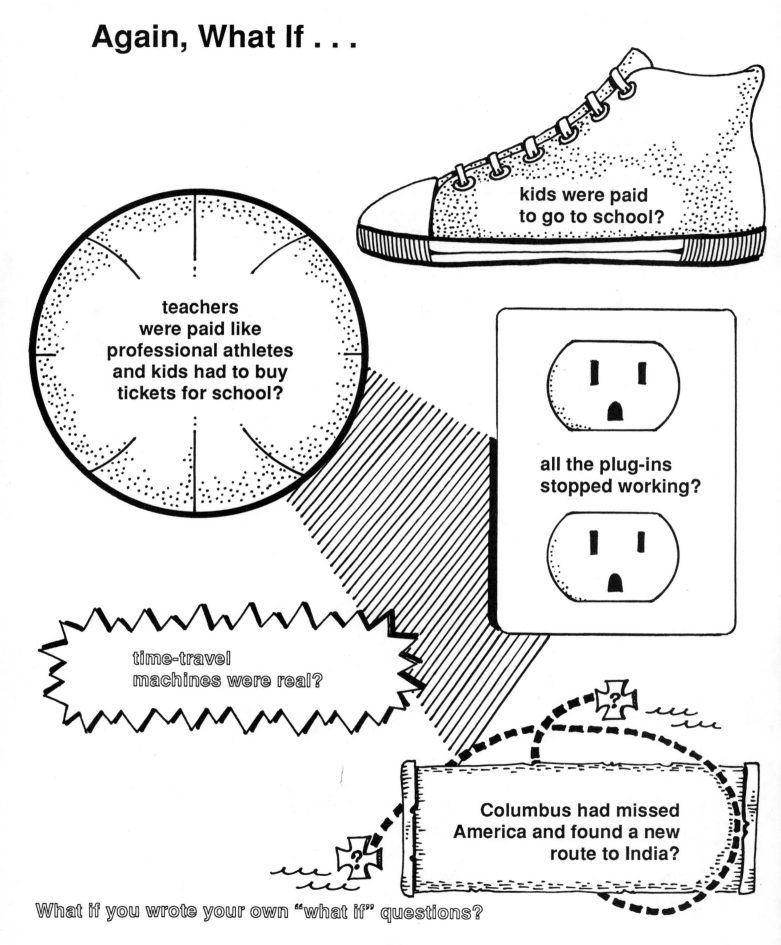

kids were paid
to go to school?

teachers
were paid like
professional athletes
and kids had to buy
tickets for school?

all the plug-ins
stopped working?

time-travel
machines were real?

Columbus had missed
America and found a new
route to India?

What if you wrote your own "what if" questions?

56

GA1489

Friendships

What does a snail say while riding on a turtle?

Wheeee!

Create some captions.

INK

A bird in a cap hidden on a cat's top hat.

A pesky spider on a pachyderm's parasol.

Think of other strange friendships. Draw some and write more captions.

GA1489

Far-Out Space
The Beginning of Three Short Space Stories

It came from Atrex from the constellation Re on the edge of Solmag's space . . .

A round, soft green glow frolicked from corner to floor to wall to corner again. It seemed to be traveling on threads of light. It stopped suddenly and . . .

When I was awakened by a piercing screech, I was bound to a half bed, half chair in what appeared to be a space . . .

GA1489

Thinking About Me and Myself

Me and Myself

To Students:

In this unit you will be thinking about, describing, and sharing things about yourself and sometimes others.

Let's try to follow these simple rules.
- Be honest.
- Be positive.
- Be accepting.
- Be kind to yourself and others.

To Teachers:

In this unit your students will be sharing their concepts and perceptions of themselves and sometimes others. Encourage them to follow the rules above. Also, allow them an option to "pass" (not respond publicly).

Here are a few teaching rules you may find helpful:
- Be honest.
- Be positive.
- Be accepting.
- Always have the option to "pass."
- Be encouraging.
- Withhold judgement.
- Participate yourself.

Suggestion: Several of the activities in this unit lend themselves to "guess who," either in small groups or for the class. For the best results have the students do the activity first, then ask or announce that you would like to read some of the students' papers to the group, display them, or have other students read them. Ask if any students object to their papers being shared. If a student objects, respect the objection; remove the paper and proceed.

Other uses:
- Journal writing
- Stems for class discussion
- Interest centers
- Paper airplane contest

Remember, as a teacher you have a moral, ethical, and professional obligation to each student, your class, and your school. Have fun and appreciate the uniqueness of each of your students.

GA1489

Favorites

My favorite foods are

_____

_____

and _____ .

My favorite color is

_____ .

My favorite TV show is

_____ .

My favorite sport is

_____ .

My favorite subject in school

is _____ .

My favorite season is . . . Circle one.

Spring   **Summer**   **Autumn**   **Winter**

Briefly explain your choice.

_____

61

GA1489

Favorite People

A List of My Five Favorite People

_____

_____

_____

_____

_____

Use this list to complete the attached statements.

I would most like to be like

_____.

I would most like to be marooned on a desert isle with

_____.

I would like to spend an hour

with _____

doing _____.

I would like to talk

to _____

about _____

_____.

These are my favorite people because they are

_____

_____

_____

_____

_____.

Favorite and Unfavorite

	My Most Favorite	My Least Favorite
day of the week	is _____ .	is _____ .
month of the year	is _____ .	is _____ .
book	is _____ .	is _____ .
cartoon or comic strip	is _____ .	is _____ .
singer	is _____ .	is _____ .
song	is _____ .	is _____ .
flower	is _____ .	is _____ .
time of the day	is _____ .	is _____ .
number	is _____ .	is _____ .
letter in the alphabet	is _____ .	is _____ .
bird	is _____ .	is _____ .
animal	is _____ .	is _____ .
pet	is _____ .	is _____ .
weather	is _____ .	is _____
politician	is _____ .	is _____ .
sound	is _____ .	is _____ .
smell	is _____ .	is _____ .
age	is _____ .	is _____ .
sight	is _____ .	is _____ .
shape	is _____ .	is _____ .

GA1489

Like Me?

Do I like me?
Well, let me see.

I'm as good
I'm as smart
I'm as capable
as I can be
for me.

And if I am
like I say I be.

Good, smart and capable
as I can be—for me.
Then yes,
Yessiree
I'm very fond of
the three of me.
                    TC

GA1489

The Me Maze

This maze is about me. When I am finished, it's me I'll see.

Start here.   Write a word or phrase in each blank.

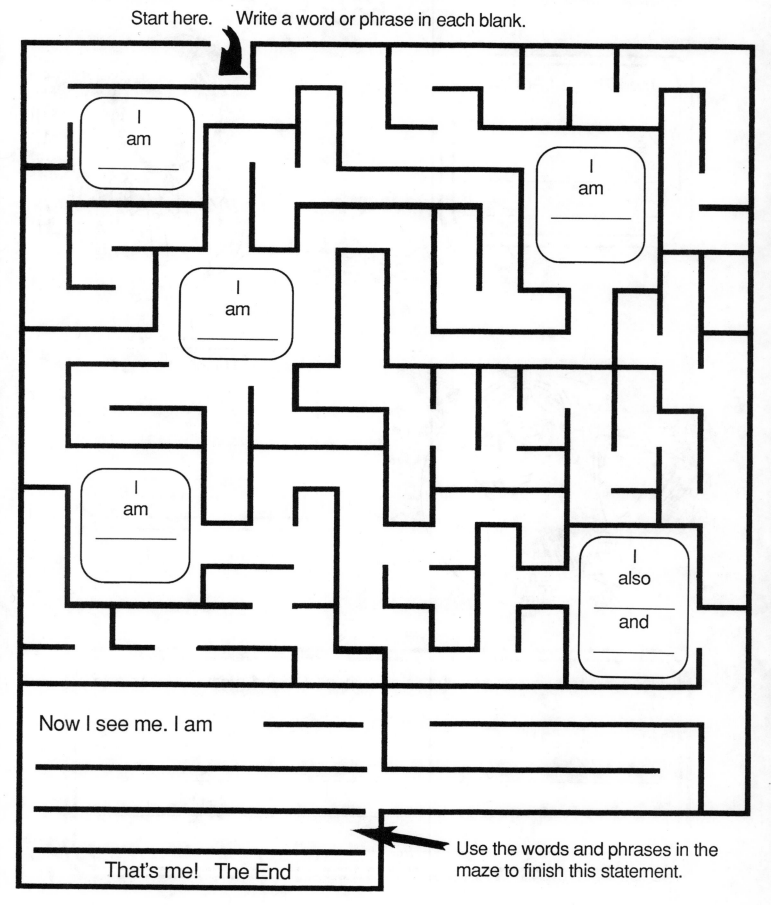

I
am
_____

I
am
_____

I
am
_____

I
am
_____

I
also
_____
and
_____

Now I see me. I am _____ _____

_____

_____

That's me!   The End

Use the words and phrases in the maze to finish this statement.

65

GA1489

More About Me

Three Things I Am Proud of

_____

_____

_____

Three Things I Like to Do

_____

_____

_____

Use your two lists and finish this statement. I would most like people to know that I . . .

_____

_____

_____

_____

Being Me

Things I Am Good At

_____

_____

_____

_____

_____

_____

_____

_____

_____

Things I Am Not Good At

_____

_____

_____

_____

_____

_____

_____

_____

_____

Here are some things that I wish I could do better.

_____   _____

_____   _____

_____

Someday I would like to be . . .

_____

Then I could . . .

_____

GA1489

Time Line

This is a time line of your life. It starts with the day you were born, ends with the present, and has several points in between. At each point describe and date each of these important occurrences. (Hint: Use your family as a resource.)

When your time line is completed you may wish to display it on your desk or a bulletin board.

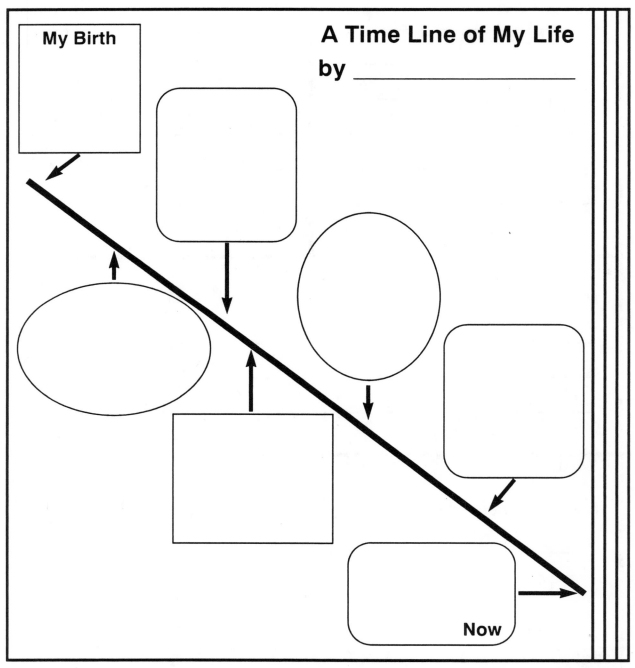

Idea as used by Rebecca Keim
5th Grade Transition Teacher
Cahokia School District
Cahokia, Illinois

GA1489

From Now Till Then

On this time line think, imagine, and dream about your future. Write when (*either how old you will be or the year*) and what you think or hope you will be doing. Start with *now* and go to *then*. (*Then is whenever you choose to stop.*)

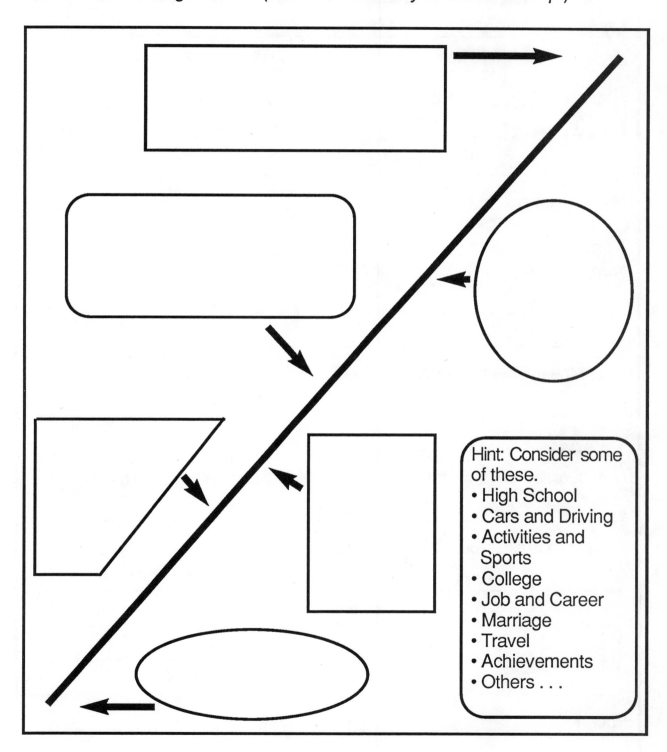

Hint: Consider some of these.
- High School
- Cars and Driving
- Activities and Sports
- College
- Job and Career
- Marriage
- Travel
- Achievements
- Others . . .

My Vita

My name is _____. Phone (_____) _____ – _____

My address is _____

_____ ZIP code _____

I am in the _____ grade at _____ school.

My favorite subject is _____. I also like _____

and _____. My grades are _____.

My hobbies are _____

_____.

I am involved in the following activities:

_____

_____.

I have the following work experience:

_____

_____.

I am qualified for and interested in the following position of employment:

_____.

The persons listed below know me and will provide references:

_____   _____

_____   _____

_____   _____

_____   _____

Phone _____   Phone _____

Viva

Make a list of things that you think you need to live.

_____   _____

_____   _____

_____   _____

_____   _____

_____   _____

_____   _____

_____   _____

Look at this list. Separate the things into these two categories:
(A) need to survive (B) want, but not necessary to survive

Draw something to represent or write a short statement about the most important thing you need and the most important thing you want.

Need	Want

Which one of the above is the most important to you? _____

Explain _____

Optional Activities

for

Things That You Need

Think of exactly ten things you would need if you were

> visiting your best friend for a week.

> lost in a desert.

> on a five-day hike through the mountains.

> vacationing for two weeks on the seashore.

> alone on a deserted island.

> on a trip to your town in the year 1900 or 2100. (Choose one.)

> going on a one-month space flight.

Create your own.

> _____

_____

Thinking About Writing and Using My Imagination

GA1489

74

Writing and Using My Imagination

To Students:

Sometimes, when you are asked to write something creative, it is difficult to think of ideas. Remember, you are creative. Everyone is to some degree. In this section you will discover a creative tool called synthesis. Synthesis makes being creative easier.

To Teachers:

This section introduces a creative structure called morphological synthesis and provides some stems and activities that assist creative thinking, writing, and inventing.

Creative thinking is enhanced by structure. For example, consider the following directions for a classroom activity.

Direction 1. Write or think about something unusual.

Direction 2. Write or think of a story about an unusual pet that can run very fast, become invisible, and is always getting you into trouble.

Direction 2 will typically generate more creative application than Direction 1. Why? Because Direction 2 provides students with information about circumstances and/or expected outcomes. It is important to provide a structure and process that will encourage creative potential.

Important Note:

The activities in this unit focus upon brainstorming, attribute listing, associating, forced fit, and synthesizing. It is important to teach students the name of the process along with the process.

Suggestions:

• Adapt or include these activities in your classroom writing instruction.
• Use these activities in learning centers.
• Try some of the activities as small group or partner assignments.
• Suggest that the students use them for making origami figures.

Remember this simple Bob Stanish instruction: "Creativity has structure."

Beginnings and Endings

Once upon a time someone suggested that a good story always has a clever beginning and a surprise ending. Since that time everyone has written happily ever after.

Think of clever beginnings. Write some of them here.

Choose a beginning;

add a middle;

then choose an ending. You have written a story.

Think of surprise endings. Write some of them here.

Many Story Parts and Then Some

There are many parts to a story. There is usually a beginning, middle, and end. Stories have settings (time and place), characters (main and supporting), and events (minor and major). Below are lists of some of these story parts.

Look at the lists. Do you think they will help you write a story? Not all the parts are here. Use your imagination to develop the missing parts.

Place	Time	Main Character	Event
1. school	1. today	1. boy	1. won a ____
2. home	2. tomorrow	2. girl	2. lost a ____
3. park	3. yesterday	3. father	3. tied for a ____
4. trip	4. in the past	4. mother	4. overcame a ___
5. farm	5. 1 year ago	5. grandfather	5. was frightened by _
6. ranch	6. 10 years ago	6. grandmother	6. was delighted when _____
7. village	7. 100 years ago	7. alien	7. was happy when ____
8. town	8. 1000 years ago	8. animal	8. was sad when __
9. city	9. in the future	9. best friend	9. met a strange __
10. planet	10. in 1 year	10. evil enemy	10. found a magic __
11. mountains	11. in 20 years	11. man	11. had an exciting __
12. desert	12. in 30 years	12. woman	12. had a funny ____
13. ocean	13. in 100 years	13. fish	13. was surprised by ___
14. forest	14. when time was not	14. bird	14. an unexpected visit to ____
15. other	15. other	15. other	15. other
_____	_____	_____	_____
_____	_____	_____	_____
_____	_____	_____	_____

Choose a place, a time, a main character, and an event.
Write your choices below.

Place _____   Time _____

Character _____   Event _____

> Note: If you have difficulty choosing, write four numbers between 1 and 15. Use the numbers to choose place, time, character, and event. You can also do this just to create a new story.

The process you have just completed is called morphological synthesis. You may call it synthesis for short.

This is the story I wrote using morphological synthesis.

Unit 8

Thinking About Expressions and Impressions

Expressions

Personalized license plates are a popular way of expressing oneself. Someday you may have your very own car. You will be given a choice of buying a license with random numbers and letters or, for an additional fee, you may design your own.

Using the outlines on the next page, design personalized license plates that you would like to have on your car. Try several before deciding on one. Have fun!

Rules:
• You may use letters, numbers, or letters and numbers in combinations.
• You may use only seven numbers and/or letters.
• Your vanity plate must be unique (one of a kind).
• If you use only letters, the cost is $100.00.*
• If you use one or more numbers the cost is $50.00.*

Have you ever seen a personalized license plate that made you smile? One that I saw lately said "IMA 10". I smiled.

*Personalized license plate prices will vary from state to state.

This page is for designing personalized license plates.

Write your state's name here. →   Date →

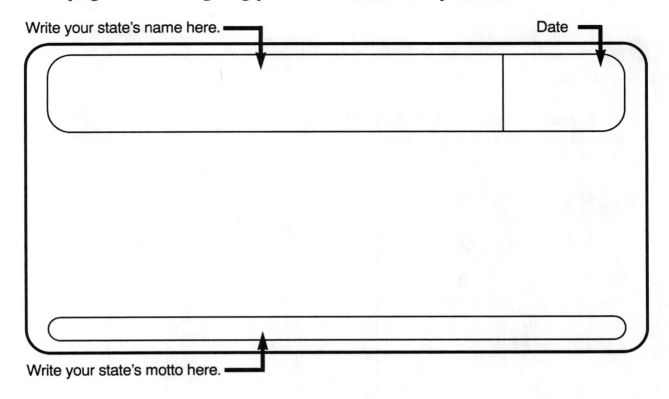

Write your state's motto here. →

Write your state's name here. →   Date →

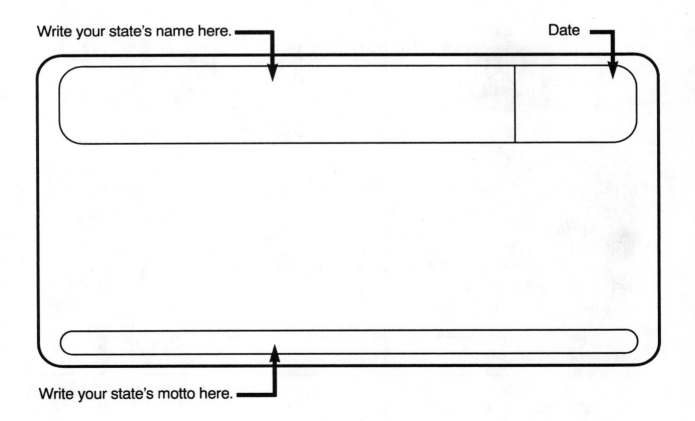

Write your state's motto here. →

GA1489

Expressions Continued

Another way to express oneself is to use a bumper sticker. A bumper sticker has a brief message, slogan, or thought. It may be serious, persuasive, factual, or humorous.

It takes talent to write a bumper sticker because of the limited space. You must say what you mean to say with as few words as possible. Also, the sticker must be readable from a distance.

Let's design and write some bumper stickers.

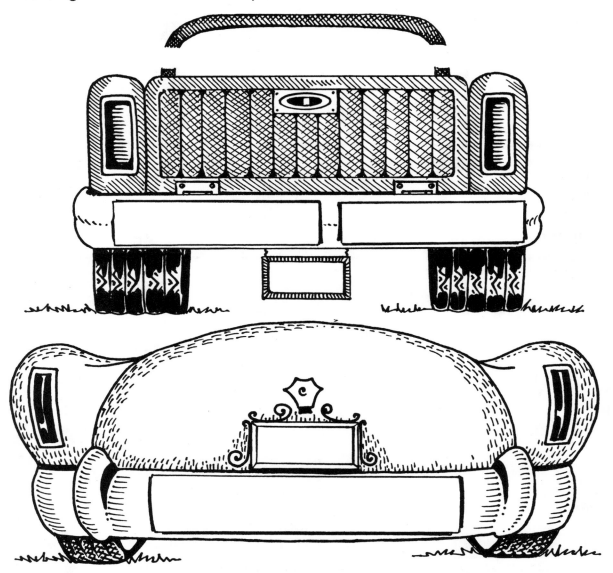

Hint: Standard letter-size sheets of uncut peel-off label paper are available from office supply stores. These sheets may be used for designing and applying the students' bumper stickers.

GA1489

This page is for creating bumper stickers.

A Bumper Sticker for a Bike

A Bumper Sticker for My School

A Bumper Sticker for a _____

A Bumper Sticker for a _____

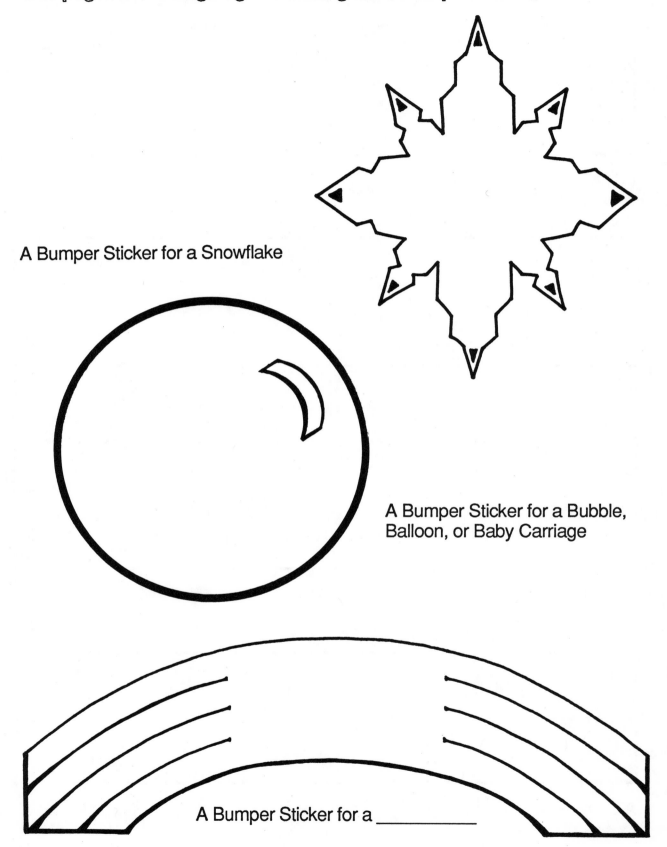

A Bumper Sticker for a Snowflake

A Bumper Sticker for a Bubble, Balloon, or Baby Carriage

A Bumper Sticker for a _____

84

Other Expressions

The way you dress, wear your hair, talk, and the music you like are other ways of expressing yourself. Can you name more?

This space is for expressing ways to express yourself.

85

GA1489

Impressive Things

Giant Trees

Rainbows

Clouds

Flowers

Sunsets

Stars

Magical Rings

Skyscrapers

Bridges

Add some things that impress you to the lists. Talk about them.

Impression

Look at the figure in the center of the page for 60 seconds. Let your mind wander; then write your thoughts.

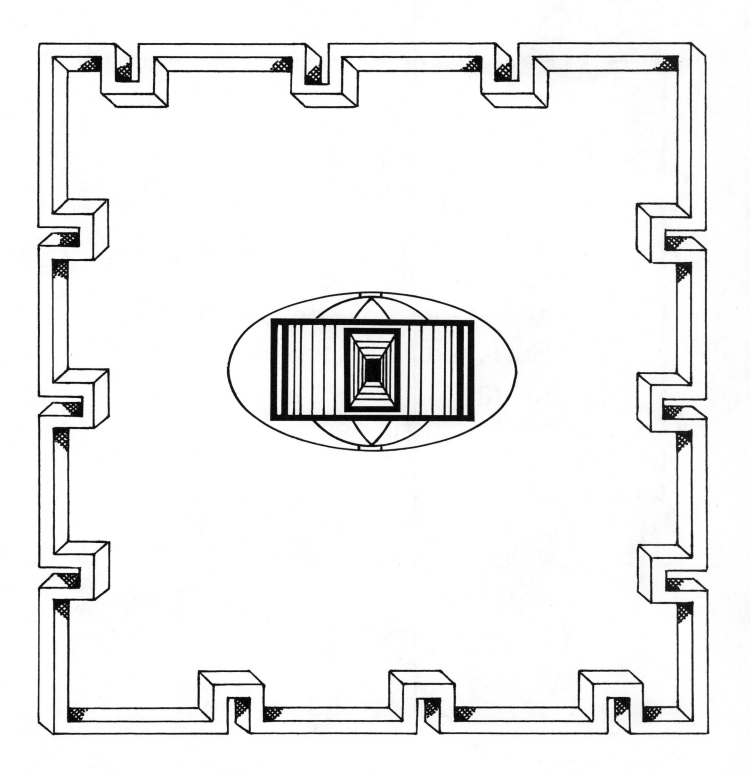

87

I think thinking's fun.
I often have to think
just to get things done.
Sometimes
I sit and think and think
and then I think some more.
But when I think too hard,
too much, too fast;
my little brain gets sore.

I've finished *Minding Minutes with Minute Minders*.
Hope you enjoy it.

GA1489

Prologue

If you were interested enough to buy this book, you probably are using your own creative ideas in your classroom.

Keep up the good work and continue minding those special minutes.

Troy

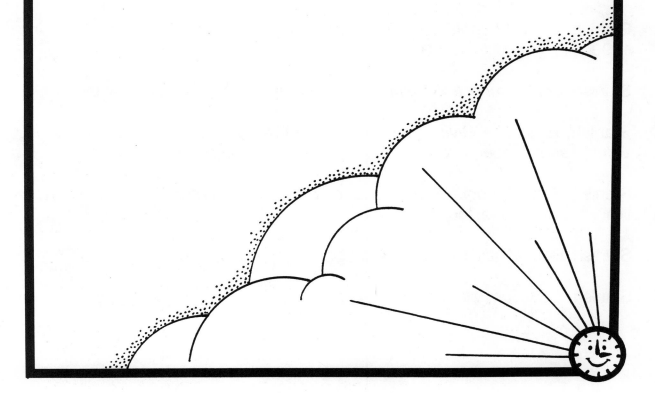

GA1489

References and Suggested Readings

Cole, Troy W. *Figure 8 Animals*. Carthage, Illinois: Good Apple, 1993.

Cole, Troy. "Minute Minders." *Challenge*, 1990-1992, Vol. 9 (1)-Vol. 12 (5).

Eberle, Bob. *Scamper: Games for Imagination Development*. Buffalo, New York: D.O.K. Publishers, 1971.

Eberle, Bob, and Bob Stanish. *CPS for Kids: A Resource Book for Teaching Creative Problem-Solving to Children*. Buffalo, New York: D.O.K. Publishers, 1980.

Raths, Louis E., Merrill Harman, and Sidney B. Simon. *Values and Teaching*. rev. ed. Columbus, Ohio: Charles E. Merrill Publishing Co., 1977.

Saint-Exupery, Antoine de. *The Little Prince*. New York: Harcourt, Brace & World, 1943.

Stanish, Bob. *Ac'cents and Ascendings*. Carthage, Illinois: Good Apple, Inc., 1990.

Stanish, Bob. *Connecting Rainbows*. Carthage, Illinois: Good Apple, Inc., 1982.

Stanish, Bob. *The Giving Book: Creative Classroom Approaches to Caring, Valuing and Cooperating*. Carthage, Illinois: Good Apple, Inc., 1988.

Stanish, Bob. *Hippogriff Feathers: Encounters with Creative Thinking*. Carthage, Illinois: Good Apple, Inc., 1981.

Stanish, Bob. *Mindanderings*. Carthage, Illinois: Good Apple, Inc., 1990.

Stanish, Bob. *Sunflowering*. Carthage, Illinois: Good Apple, Inc., 1986.